The Pathology of Emotions

Copyright 2017

By

Gregory A. Hill

Published in the United States by

Gregory A. Hill Publishing Co.

Houston, TX

Book Cover Design by

Gregory A. Hill

Email:gahill22@yahoo.com

Table of Contents

Introduction - Pg. 4

The Pathology of Emotions -Pg. 7

My Pain, My Path, My cure- Pg. 9

But You Didn't Remember It - Pg. 19

Childhood… Lost - Pg. 24

Marriage, the Final Frontier - Pg. 29

Shhh…Listen - Pg. 35

A New Program - Pg. 43

The Monster(s) Within - Pg. 46

Mentoring Dynamics - Pg. 49

No Words Necessary - 51

The Pathology of Emotions

Introduction

This little booklet is another step along the way in my ongoing efforts to help bring about social change by helping people with individual, personal change. Its' purpose is to get more to the core of **_why_** people do what they do-or better yet, why do people do things they know they shouldn't. In my previous books, <u>My Father, This Side of Heaven</u>, and <u>The _Other_ Lost Boys</u>, I presented perspective one and two on the subject of trauma and dysfunctional family relationships, as they relate to our troubled youth. Consider this step as perspective three. The content of these three books largely reflects the experience of nearly 40 years of mentoring.

There's a growing movement in today's society encouraging people to learn their family heritage and ancestry. For whatever value or wholeness one might find in that, might I suggest we put even more effort in researching our recent and current history- from childhood until now- making that <u>"quest to know why we are emotionally and mentally the way we are"</u>, even more meaningful and complete. For most of us, our present day relationships and day to day experiences have affected our lives in a much more profound way than our ancestry has.

Hopefully this script will create a desire to research, examine, and move from where you are to where you need and want to be. So buckle up and take this short journey with me, and hopefully in the end, you are better able to recognize and treat any unhealthy areas in your pathology that may need to be "adjusted", in order to live the life you long for, and the life you, your friends, and loved ones deserve.

If you have read my previous books, you may be thinking "here we go again, making excuses for peoples' bad behavior." As I have stated in previous writings, this is in no way an effort to excuse bad behavior. The goal here is to understand the source of the dysfunctional behavior, then finding a path to repairing it. In order to do that, we must find a way to bring light to, uncover, and adequately treat, the root causes (pathology) of the unhealthy behavior, and begin repairing it.

What I do believe is this, the majority of the bad decisions that affect our important relationships and our community, are primarily a result of the pain and trauma of damaged emotions and relationships.

If you have read any of my previous two books, you already know that I have mentored countless numbers of young men and their stories are sometimes chilling. Well, let me introduce you to the pathology of this one:

From M.C.- (a former juvenile resident)

For starters, I was molested as a child when I was around five years old. When I started school, the bullying started to creep in. By the 6th grade I was getting bullied from the first day of school. Most of the kids always laughed at my clothes while at the bus stop because I rarely had any new clothes at the start of the school year. I actually can't ever remember going shopping for school clothes. The next year in 7th grade, those same bullies were right there to bully me again.

My English teacher, that same year, told me that I wasn't smart enough for English class and that I would never make it out of the 7th grade…but I proved her wrong.

Girls would call me ugly, I endured many racial slurs, and I got into fights, which was just an extension of all I was going through. In addition to those things, there were issues at home where my parents were breaking up, and often being emotionally degraded and beat down by my father. Then the kids at church treated me much the same way as my classmates did. By the eighth grade I was emotionally broken into pieces.

*Needless to say, I didn't have much of a childhood at all and I found myself still playing with 7-year-old's toys at the age of 12. There were many times when my father would physically degrade and abuse me in front of my friends, for no reason at all. After my parents divorced I found myself with nowhere to stay. My father's new wife, (who barely knew me), didn't like me so when I found myself homeless, she didn't want me in their house so I had to sleep in the car outside -in the cold.   I have always felt like an unwanted child.**

These were just a few of the "highlights" of his childhood, or shall I say, this was part of his pathology, and believe me, there is much more. He was forced to walk a treacherous "path" that he had virtually no control over. As of this writing, he is making progress but there is still a long, hard road to healing ahead.

The Pathology of Emotions

Pa·thol·o·gy - (pă-thŏl′ə-jē)*n.*

1. The scientific study of the nature of disease and its causes, processes, development, and consequences. **2.** The anatomic or functional manifestations of a disease: *the pathology of cancer.***3.** A departure or deviation from a normal condition:

When we have physical pains or diseases that we cannot cure ourselves, we typically make a trip to the doctor, looking for a solution. The root cause and progression of that disease leaves a "trail", or path of dysfunction, causing a physical symptom. That trail is typically referred to as the pathology of the disease. As in all diagnostic procedures, the first goal should be trying to find the root cause of the problem-the "where it all started."

For most of us, that word "pathology" is usually associated with physical conditions. It never occurred to me until recently that the concept applies to our emotional condition as well. My goal is to take a look at some of the key ingredients that make up our emotional pathology. That "path of logic" will have a great effect on ones' view of the world around them, the people they love and interact with, and most of the decisions they make.

How many bad decisions have you made because of emotional stress, knowing that was it was not the wisest thing, but something that made you feel good, get revenge, or relieve the pain for the moment? It perhaps soothed the intense, immediate pain, followed up by the 'subconscious' thought of, "I'll worry about the consequences later."

In the case of physical or emotional trauma, the pathology must be uncovered, noting that often the two come in the same package.

When one has a flesh wound, such as a knife cut or

severe bruise, the open wound is very obvious because of the visual tissue damage and or bleeding. Once the wound heals, a scar forms and the pain of the wound begins to fade away. However, if someone were to 'jab' that wound while it is still fresh or not yet healed, the wounded person would have a negative reaction from the touch, directly related to the level of healing that has taken place.

One of the most notable diseases we are all familiar with is cancer. As the disease spreads, and more severe symptoms appear, the cause and the type of cancer usually becomes clear. In some cases, early detection increases the chances of it being treated and cured. There are various types, cures, and treatments for cancer, necessary simply because people and their types of cancer are different. Therefore, I believe damaged emotions must be viewed and handled in a similar way, on a case by case basis.

My Path, My Pain, My Cure

Consider this. Go into the woods and pick out a large oak tree to sketch. Now picture 99 other people surrounding the same tree, doing the same thing. Even though they are all drawing the exact same tree, each person's sketch of the tree will be different from the others. I believe that same principle is in play when it comes to treating our emotional problems-our emotional cancers.

Just as the drawings of that tree will appear different to each artist, so too will there s o m e t i m e s be different reactions and cures experienced by each person who is treated for their individual problems. Therefore, all people who deal with the same trauma are not necessarily going to react and handle it the exact same way. Although there are basic treatments that apply to almost all, each person has their own individual catalog of coping mechanisms and ways of healing-or ways of easing their pain.

Even though in every case there are basic things that usually apply to all, it is so vitally important to recognize and accept that a persons' individuality will make the final determination of how to analyze, respond to, and repair their emotional issues.

Imagine there are two pick-up trucks preparing to do the same job. Each one is loaded with the same load, and will take the same path to their dump sites. Both trucks outwardly are exactly the same; the same in color, engine **size**, tires, and exterior and interior accessories. When put to the test, truck "A" conquered the hilly terrain and reached its destination with no problem. Meanwhile, truck "B" never made it to the top of the hill before his engine failed. What was the difference?

Because we judged from only the outside appearance, and didn't realize that truck "A" had a diesel engine and truck

"B" had a gasoline engine, we totally misjudged and mistreated the situation. Until we consider all of the individual factors, internal as well as external, we are likely to misjudge the diagnosis, possibly missing the needed treatment.

Those traits, along with family relationships, physical and or mental handicaps, "second-tier" relationships, the media, overall environment, and last but not least, our unique personality, will largely determine the best treatment for each individual.

I believe that nearly all of us have experienced some level of trauma and anxiety in our lives, since no one's life is perfect. To that extent, the "average person", (whatever that means), comes into this world equipped with a level of ability to handle some level of trauma in their lives.

Often, emotional wounds are often ignored, denied, or "misdiagnosed" by the injured person. They pretend those wounds don't exist, or convince themselves that they have gotten over them. Eventually, someone, or something, will unknowingly "touch that invisible wound," and the resulting pain often leads to the beginning of dysfunctional relationships, or anti-social behavior.

Probably most of you have seen or heard of the TV show "Criminal Minds". The show centers on the Behavioral Analysis Unit, (BAU), a department of the Federal Bureau of Investigation. The main tactic of the "BAU" is to use behavioral-based training and research to solve complex crimes. These analyses will enable agents to examine a suspects' past and present habits and actions, or pathology, to get an idea of likely future behavior that will aid in solving the crimes.

I believe that with proper diagnosis and treatment, we have the capability to heal, or at least manage the bad experiences that have affected our lives. As you know by now, it is my contention that few of us, if any, can do it alone.

I would like to take a moment to examine what I believe are several major areas of life that help to weave t h e   p a t h   o f   each persons' individual pathology.

Environment-The place where we grow up,-our surroundings, is where it all starts. Since we are more affected by what we see and experience first-hand, the people, places and things that a re a part of our daily lives usually have the greatest influence on how we see and process most of the experiences we have. Almost without exception, the house where we were raised, (and more specifically, what goes on inside that house), gets the first crack at forming who and what we have faith in, what's good or bad, right or wrong, clean and unclean, and so on and so on. How often does abuse, parental discord, and overall household dysfunction shape our views of life, love, relationships, etc., and ultimately our decision-making?

Recently, as I was walking into a Walmart, I passed a man wearing a T-shirt with a saying on it that made me laugh. It illustrated what I just said. It simply read- "If you knew my family, you would understand."

The second phase of your environment, your neighborhood/community, u s u a l l y has the next most powerful influence on how you see life, especially as a child. As I noted in previous writings, the "neighborhood" can, at times, overcome the influence of the best of households.

For all of us, particularly adolescents, the desire to "belong and "fit in", is at, or near the top of our l i f e ' s p r i o r i t i e s ,   o f t e n   l e a d i n g   t o   t h i n g s   that w i l l   i n f l u e n c e   our self- esteem and personal relationships. By the way, it is noted by many that the feeling of being loved and a sense of belonging is the major lure that gets most people into gangs. Then, the gang basically becomes the new "parents and siblings." Along with those new parents a n d   s i b l i n g s   c o m e s   a new sense of belonging a n d   u s u a l l y   a new perspective on life. Remember, we all naturally want to please our "parents." Thus, a new set of rules come into place that influence decision making and relationships. Their "path-of-logic" has taken a new course-one which they believe will bring what they long for-love and acceptance. Unfortunately, it is only a shadow of the real thing.

Education-Dysfunctional families have played a significant role in the educational system for two reasons. First, the home life of far too many students is so disruptive and traumatic that many of the important social skills that were previously taught at home have largely disappeared, i.e. respect for elders, common courtesy, and discipline. In turn, when much of that dysfunction is played out at school, our laws no longer allow the implementation of very many effective or corrective disciplinary measures to address the situations. The resulting behaviors affect the entire school environment.

Secondly, those dysfunctional children have a much more difficult time focusing and giving enough attention to classwork and learning. That results in more and more students being "labeled", demoted, and suspended, as well as more of them are graduating with sub-par educations, if they graduate at all.

-Years ago while riding the bus home from work, I overheard a young mother talking about her child's behavior at school. Her attitude was, "no teacher will ever (p h y s i c a l l y) discipline my child." It took all of the strength in me to keep my composure and my mouth shut. I so desperately wanted to reply, "If that's your attitude then fine, keep that little so-and-so home and teach him yourself".

(Forgive me, I'm still living in the dark ages where it wasn't against the law for teachers to discipline students, where the adults ran the classroom, and the students did not decide the dress code. Schools are now faced with the additional tasks of overcoming the effects of the students' lives at home/neighborhood, often having to teach things that should be taught, and reinforced, at home).

Okay, I'm back to reality now.

This "reduced quality" of public education that many children in our public school systems are receiving today is not doing a good enough job of preparing them for the life ahead. That, along with an injection of what I would call a dissolving set of moral values in society in general, which I believe is at the forefront of "broken" homes, helps create the pathway for mental and emotional chaos. That usually results a display of various areas of social dysfunction. As a result, in my opinion, it seems that many children are getting high school diplomas with what amounts to a seventh or eighth-grade educations. Now, their "path to a successful life", is very likely to be very narrow and limited, sometimes leading to frustration, and the behavior that follows it.

Exposure-In my dealings with teenagers, it seems that fewer and fewer stray far from home after finishing high school, particularly in the minority communities. Not only are they not exposed to other places and cultures, but often far-reaching parts of their own city are never explored. That lack of exposure is not limited only to other places, different people, and different cultures, but also to the vast array of careers and job opportunities.

Therefore many of these opportunities go unnoticed and unknown to this core of people. It is then reasonable to understand that when all a person sees and knows (outside of the television perhaps), is what is around them, it limits their goals and dreams… and becomes a stepping stone, or rather, a "missing" stone in their pathology.

Upon reflection, I too was a "victim" of lack of exposure. While growing up I discovered I was a decent sketch artist. In high school my exposure to drafting, as well as a fascination with building design, led me to aspire to be an architect. So, off the college I went. I was soon informed that that particular college offered no degrees in architecture, but there was a field of study called "Landscape Architecture". Partially because my carefree mindset at the time, and not having a 'backup plan", I signed up for a field of study that I had absolutely no knowledge of, and had never even heard of! Fortunately, I caught on, graduated, and it has allowed me to afford a good life.

Esteem (Of Self)-Needless to say, this is a biggie. Unfortunately, it is one of the least understood-particularly in how it affects one's decision making process. The view that we have of ourselves, how we think we measure up, how we think we look to others, and where we fit in, are some of the major factors that come into play when we make certain decisions.

** My personal experience was that I grew up with very poor self-esteem. I was mostly an "A" student in school, but outside of my academic success, my view of myself left much to be desired. By middle school I was going through a "chubby" phase, and was constantly told, "You are going to be fat, just like your daddy." Thirdly, the slightest misstep in any endeavor was followed by the phrase, "that boy has book-sense, but no common sense." Even though I never accepted the "no common sense" notion, it still took its toll on me emotionally.*

Later on in high school, after I had lost some weight, I came to a point where I simply began to re-evaluate "me". I am not sure where it came from but I began to view myself differently. I began to say to myself, "hey, you're okay, you're good-looking enough", etc. It took a year or two, but my view of myself changed, and of course, up went my self-esteem.

The pathology that was in my mind was redirected, and I began to interact with life and people differently. I had to undo the pathology of my own perception of myself, and/or one that was put on me. One of the main benefits gained from my new-found self-esteem was that I would now approach a pretty girl with much less apprehension-thus a new perspective in that area of decision making because of a "healing" in my pathology.*

Remember, a single traumatic event can have a powerful effect on one's emotional pathology- and lets' not forget repeated, long-lasting traumatic events.

Exclusive strengths and gifts-(your persona, your perception of your life's experiences)

In the midst of desperate times, difficult decisions often come down to possibilities/probabilities in terms of consequences and reactions. At an early stage of hunger, one might decide that the possibility of going to jail for stealing from a grocery store is not worth the risk. At an advanced stage of hunger, the probability of getting caught may be the same, but that probability becomes much less of a factor, since the growling stomach pains have moved to center stage. Now the decision-maker has a new, more powerful driving force-survival. Right and wrong begin to fade in the distance, with starvation taking the lead role.

Often when I talk to people, a typical reaction is, "when you know the difference between right and wrong, and understand the consequences of your actions, there is no excuse for bad choices or unlawful behavior. As the song form the screen-play *"Porgy and Bess"* says, "Well, it ain't necessarily So". I can assure you that virtually all of those people who believe that have never felt trauma that took them to the edge of death, the brink of insanity, or the doorstep of suicide. And that situation is much more devastating for young people. After exhausting all **known** possibilities, how desperate would you have to get before you would steal food, respond violently to an abusive spouse,…or (<u>fill in the blank</u>)?

Over the years, as I hear of the many horrendous things people do, particularly very young people, I am beginning to understand why persons so young could even think of some of those things.

I am reminded of a news story I read about a decade ago. Two 12-year-old boys had been labeled cold-hearted killers, seemingly having no conscience at all. They had murdered more than once, and had absolutely no remorse about it. Are you going to pass that off as, "Oh well, they were just bad, stupid kids.' Even though I don't know their story (pathology), I will bet you all the tea in China, that if you knew their story, (and/or lived it yourself), you would probably vomit, and at least plead for mercy in their sentencing and treatment.

There are so many children subjected to unspeakable horrors and the only way they have of coping is to fight back in an equally horrific way. At least wait until you hear their story…their pathology…before you pass final judgement.

I have personally talked to teens whose situations were almost unbearable to listen to. Two young men were desperate to find a solution to the abuse the family was taking at the hands of their father. After exhausting every possibility they had at their disposal, they were at their wits end, with no legal solution in sight. They virtually looked to me for a solution other than their last idea-to murder their father. I did not have one. (Just saying "tough it out" was not an option).

I talked to a judge about it and the judges' response was, "Mr. Hill, the system is just broken." They had no legal recourse, so the only option they could see was to resort to violence. Fortunately, circumstances changed and a serious tragedy was averted.

What is also incredible about the situation is that the son still loves his dad! As a matter of fact, he even visits him in prison and sends him money that he should be paying rent with!

As twisted as that situation may sound, it just shows how strong a father-son relationship can be.

There are other contributing factors that affect healthy emotional development as we grow up. Below are a few samples:

-Constant disappointment- a separated parent who promises to spend the weekend with the child, but consistently is a now-show.
-Total abandonment.

-A home where there are various forms of abuse.

-A life of constantly moving from place to place, never experiencing a stable, wholesome, living environment;

-A family that is broken through parental separation, resulting in the child having to go back and forth from parent to parent. Perhaps even worse, when the single parent "entertains" a parade of "partners", married or not, including a host of half brothers and sisters-creating a lot of emotional confusion. (Often this leads to the parent having to eventually choose "allegiance" to the newest partner or their child, who is trying to sort out their position in the family tree.

-A situation where a child is emotionally "split down the middle" by the parents' divorce, or by a parent that "keeps a child on the fence" by not being completely in or completely out of their life.

These types of circumstances often have the emotional

effect of ripping the child down the middle. Any combination of these elements typically leads to a child that is very insecure. By this time, the typical coping mechanisms of drugs, sex, and "whatever", has become their new "path", (one that brings temporary relief), which often becomes a normal part of their life.

So, when it is all said and done, it is critical that each person's individuality, background, and pathology is sufficiently analyzed and understood before any treatment is given.

...But You Didn't Remember It

Ah, the subconscious area of the mind. As best I can define or describe it, it is an area of our brains that acts as the main-frame of all that we are and do. It is the storehouse for every experience we ever have in our lives, every- single- one, no exceptions. Fortunately, or unfortunately, the brain decides, for various reasons at various times, to hide certain experiences from our consciousness. It protects us from reliving some of the trauma of bad experiences that are often emotionally crippling.

Essentially, our lives are affected by all of our experiences all of the time, whether those experiences are good or bad. Those hidden experiences will affect and guide many of the decisions we make. It can get away with it because seldom, if ever, do we really access, acknowledge, and act on everything that lurks in the "hidden places in our minds." Unfortunately, those "hidden places" do not hide from our emotions, but rather influences them.

The science of subliminal messaging is more powerful and effective than most of us realize. Marketing experts have that art down to a science, influencing our buying habits more than most of us realize. Have you ever done something, and shortly afterward asked yourself, "Why did I do that." In many cases, the subconscious mind reacted so quickly, you didn't realize that it "wasn't you", so to speak. The subconscious mind never sleeps and never misses any data that we are exposed to, and it never goes away. Nevertheless, its "influences" can be uncovered, managed, and/or redirected.

One good example perhaps, of the viciousness of this

subtle deception might be the experiment of the frog in the boiling water. I've never done it myself, but I am told that you can put a frog in a shallow pan of water on the stove, and in gradual increments turn up the heat on the burner, and boil the frog to death, although he could have easily, at any time, just jumped out of the pan.

Here's the catch: if you turn the heat on very low at the start, the water is still comfortable and the frog won't sense any real danger.

After a short while, you can turn up the heat just one notch. The increase in temperature is so slight that the frog won't notice it. He will soon become comfortable with it. An hour or so later, repeat the process, and the frog's body/mind will once again adjust. Repeat the process over and over again, and you will boil the frog in a pot of water that he could have easily jumped out of!

I believe there are numerous areas in which we are being "led" in our subconscious mind, and not the least of these is the visual and audible aspects of our entertainment-movies, (from "A" rated to "X" rated), and music. Between the increasingly amazing cinematography at the theaters, and now even on television, we are being subtly bombarded and subtly manipulated with powerful and influential messages that, for the most part, we are totally unaware of. As years go by, our minds are undergoing a "shift in thinking' that is so slight that it is virtually undetectable-But that's another book. Do not underestimate the power of the subconscious mind!

Your brain has the power to adjust itself to untold misery, mostly by "blocking out" unpleasant experiences in order to help ease or deny emotional pain so that you can keep your sanity. But that blocking out comes with a price, and almost always at the cost of our emotional health. It allows that dysfunction to take root and grow in your soul. The deeper the root, the more difficult the up-rooting is likely to be, and often at a cost many can never pay.

Another example would be a person who eats, doesn't brush afterward and says to himself," my teeth are fine, they don't need to be brushed." Years can go by, and you never notice any problem with your teeth, until… The amount of damage that is done each day is so slight that it virtually can't be measured. But in time, the damage will show itself.

Again, your brain is your number one safety and survival mechanism. As mentioned before, it automatically attempts to find ways to adjust to any situation or adversity. It will do what it has to do in order to keep you sane or comfortable, or simply alive. One perfect example is how some people go to extremes to cope with constant, violent, physical abuse that they are a victim of or exposed to. It is documented that many women constantly fall into abusive relationships because as far back as they can remember it was something they endured almost daily. At whatever point they came to the conclusion that there is no way out, their brain now basically has three choices, fight back, (which is often deemed undoable), suicide, or submit to it-thereby, in a sense, moving it to the "normal" category of the brain, which makes the abuse "okay." The result, it doesn't 'hurt" anymore. In extreme cases, the abuse moves from abnormal to normal, and believe it or not, in some cases, the "victim" craves abuse and it eventually becomes a part of their normal, acceptable pathology-and as such, a normal part of their life.

Since all of this "makes itself at home" in one's subliminal consciousness, the long-lasting devastation can reach far and wide, affecting generations to come.

Okay, brace yourselves. I already know, some who read this will think, "This is unbelievable, what a horrible person. What kind of evil parent would do that to their child?"

-A particular parent who spent much of their childhood in foster-care, was moved around to multiple "bad" homes as a child, experiencing a similar trauma in almost every case. This person was always overlooked and was never

given the same treatment (food, goodies) as the other children in the home, and always made to feel less than, and an outsider. That grew into an enormous emotional pain that developed roots that went deep into their soul.

Upon marriage, the first child, (let's call him John), was found to be severely allergic to "apples." Eating apples would almost always result in a visit to the emergency room.

While attending a neighboring child's birthday party, guess what was on the menu-"apples". Believe it or not, when the parent "assumed" that the son was about to experience their past pain of being "left out", their 35-year-old trauma that had been repressed and gone unhealed, kicked in. That parent could not bear to watch John endure that same "left out" feeling, and proceeded to give John an apple, too! Fortunately, the other parent came to the rescue before much damage was done.

In most cases, without the help of effective therapy, the pathology never changes. In fact, it often grows like weeds and can grow deep roots in one's soul. Whatever your dysfunction is, know this one thing: you don't automatically **grow** out of it, you have to **get** out of it.

While I'm on the subject, the following is a story that I was reluctant to include because of the horrific nature of it. So, if you have a weak stomach, or even if you are just human, perhaps you should skip to the next chapter.

An evangelist related a story from a woman who was rescuing children from a child-sex ring. In some country overseas, this "brothel" featured men who would come in, get a drink of something with mind-altering drugs in it, and proceed to the child of their choice. In this case, the child of choice... was an 18-month old baby girl. (No typo-you read it right).

Although the lady eventually rescued the child, I believe that event was etched into the child's subconscious mind. As she grows older and suffers emotionally from an event that she most assuredly doesn't remember, how does she get help?

I don't know either. Unless the lady keeps track of her and informs her when she is "ABLE" to handle it…

Childhood…Lost

In the middle of talking about subliminal effects and the subconscious mind, the subject of a "lost childhood" takes center stage. As so, its deadliest weapon is its deceptive, subliminal nature. Though seldom talked about, the trauma caused by the experience of an "insufficient, or damaged childhood stage" is critical when researching, and treating, some adult behaviors.

Just as there are physical stages that must be experienced in order for a person to physically grow up properly, so too are there emotional stages that must be nourished and experienced, to bring about proper emotional health. I believe that one of the most overlooked, misunderstood, and important stages of adult emotional health is the emotional piece that comes from experiencing a "normal" childhood. I firmly believe that when a person is never allowed to "be a child", and experience the playtime, nurturing, and stable environment that is so critical, it can leave a hole in their soul that can literally be devastating.

Childhood memories are supposed to be memories of playfulness, fun, care-free thoughts, and community stability, surrounded by a sense of safety, with just enough rainy days to make one cherish the playtime. Previously, I mentioned the difficulty many people have in trying to self-diagnose. The subliminal nature of this malady puts it close to the top of that category.

A lost childhood typically results in an emotional unrest that is very confusing to the person. It creates a since of emotional emptiness that most find it difficult to figure out. Usually there is some behavioral imbalance in areas of life that usually leads to childish behaviors. Consequently, I believe that a severely damaged childhood has a significant effect on how a person matures.

Probably the most noted symptom is a yearning for things that were missed in childhood. The effects may be too numerous to count and often difficult to identify. And of course, that lacking will almost always show up in close relationships, as well as varying areas of your decision making.

If you have seen the movie "Antoine Fisher", one of the central things he talked about was the trauma of his childhood he termed "rainy days." Here was his analogy: to a child who wants to do the most natural thing of going outside to play, it is disappointing when the rain prevents that from happening. He noted that children learn very early that from time to time it will rain, and going outside to play can't happen. It can be a disappointing and sad time, but a "few' rainy days can be handled, even by a child. They can reason that it is just a part of growing up. However, when it rains too much, nearly every day, the mounting frustration can be devastating. At some point, the child simply gives up on ever going outside to play again. When that important childhood exercise and expression of life gets smothered in a child, and that "light" goes out, it has a huge, negative effect on the emotional health of a child. (In Antoine's case, his "rain" was consistent emotional and physical abuse).

As is customary, that trauma affects the adulthood. The lack of sufficient childhood time often causes significant trauma that seemingly few understand. Have you ever met any forty-year-old "teenagers?" I've met a few.

A common situation is where the oldest sibling is forced to "be a surrogate parent" to the younger siblings because the only parent has to work two jobs to "keep the lights on."

Michael Jackson, one of the greatest entertainers this century, or perhaps the world, has ever known, may be near the top of the list of examples of what can happen to a "successful" person, whose adult success came at the cost of his childhood, being robbed of sufficient childhood time and experiences. It seems to be common knowledge that once his talents were realized, he was forced to hone his entertainment skills at the "cost of being a child." As a result, there were areas of his adult behavior that many people questioned-areas that most feel were "inappropriate for his age." It is obvious that at some point he realized that he had emotional issues stemming from his childhood, or lack thereof. The following song he wrote, which is heartbreaking to listen to, expresses his realization of the main cause of his adulthood emotional struggles. Below are the lyrics. You can find the song on YouTube.

Have you seen my Childhood?
 I'm searching for the world that I come from
'Cause I've been looking around
In the lost and found of my heart...
No one understands me.
They view it as such strange eccentricities...
'Cause I keep kidding around
Like a child, but pardon me...
People say I'm not okay
'Cause I love such elementary things...
It's been my fate to compensate,
for the Childhood
I've never known...
Have you seen my Childhood?
I'm searching for that wonder in my youth
Like pirates in adventurous dreams,
Of conquests and kings on the throne.
Before you judge me, try hard to love me,
Look within in your heart then ask,
Have you seen my childhood?
People say I'm strange that way,
Cause I love such elementary things.
It's been my fate to compensate,

For the childhood I've never known.
Have you seen my childhood?
I'm searching for that wonder in my youth
Like fantastical stories to share,
The dreams I would dare,
Watch me fly…
Before you judge me, try hard to love me.
The painful youth I've had…
Have you seen my childhood?

To me, the moral of this story is, "It's been my fate to compensate, for the childhood, I've never known."

That speaks directly to something I mentioned in my previous writing, and that is the concept of how our brains adjusts to our condition in order to help us thrive, or at least survive." If we find ourselves at a severe hunger stage, our brains will –compensate-, "adjust" and allow" us, to eat foods that we once thought were disgusting. Emotionally, it works much the same way. We find ourselves doing things to try and compensate for the emotional hole in our souls- things that "under normal circumstances", would never have come into play. There are areas in our souls that must be nourished by the "emotional food" of simply being a child..

I believe that song paints a picture that says, in most cases, the pain and trauma associated with the loss of a childhood is reflected in child-like, or, "immature" behaviors. Simply because coping mechanisms vary from person to person, it can also be why it is often difficult to diagnose and treat. That leads me back to the importance of therapy, be it from a licensed professional, or the caring, attentive ear of a friend, or a mentor.

In some cases, the childhood trauma was simply a situation where a child was constantly blamed and punished by being forced to do "unnecessary and/ or inappropriate chores" for their age, and almost always at the cost of playtime. When a distraught single parent takes out their frustrations on the child, giving the child "insufficient" playtime, it can set the stage for an abnormal, unfulfilled childhood, a troubled adolescence, and a future built on shaky ground. In my opinion, there likely are only a handful of traumatic childhood experiences that are more difficult to diagnose and cure than this one-largely because of its subtlety.

Marriage, the Final Frontier

The "state of matrimony", particularly in these United States, is in big trouble. In my observation from dealing with young people, more and more of them simply have no desire, or plan, to get married. Unfortunately, much of their reasoning is sound, simple, and logical. Almost everywhere they turn, often starting with their own home, there is either a bad marriage, no marriage, or multiple marriages, all which leads them to the conclusion, "why do it at all?" Remember, what children see is much more powerful that what they are told. (Wait! That goes for adults as well…sorry)

As we all know, there are many reasons marriages fail, but I would like to point out what I believe to be the most common reason of all. In my opinion, most marriages fail because one or both parties have too much unresolved trauma in their lives. Those open, untreated emotional wounds from past traumatic experiences that were never treated and still festering inside, are usually resurrected by the intimacy of close relationships-especially marriage-and then, parenting.

Those emotional wounds were "seeds" in a sense, buried deep in the back of a person's "spiritual closet." That dark closet is filled with various items of "emotional clothing and bandages" that hides emotional scars. Those bandages come in many forms, i.e. drugs, make-up, denial, shallow relationships, false self-esteem, and on and on and on. All it takes is for those seeds to be watered with a certain close relationship, and up from one's soul sprouts the social and emotional dysfunctions (pains) that were festering in the shadows.

In most cases when couples move in together,

and/or when children enter into the mix, the hidden seeds in the dark places in the "emotional closet" get watered. Children, by their nature, will "unknowingly" find a way to "pick at the scabs", or "dig up and expose those sores" that the parent(s) didn't properly address. As many of us have found out, marriage before children often looks very different from marriage after children.

When we as humans begin to date and look for a marriage partner, the main goal should be to get to know each other to decide if that is who we should marry. It is a great plan, but the problem is that in most cases, each person only shows their "good" side. Too often, neither person knows to, or doesn't know how to, take the time to really dig deeply and really get to know and sufficiently recognize the other person's pathology. And if a defective pathology is discovered, proper action is seldom taken to correct it. In many instances, defective pathologies are purposely buried deep, often no one can find them-not even the burier.

Tragically, in today's society, when two young people meet, one, or both, is likely to be emotionally unstable because of their traumatic upbringing. They find comfort in one another because they both can understand and relate to one another's trauma. Sometimes, in an attempt to confirm their marital plans, they will go to marriage counseling, hoping to not make a marriage mistake. Unfortunately, that often is a bit too late. If they have already decided to get married, it is likely that nothing the counselor says will change their minds.

Married or not, far too often the relationship leads to intimacy, which too often leads to "parents" who aren't together very long... and here we go again. Often the most severe trauma that each one has endured is never exposed or talked about. That is usually because of one of four things:

1) The trauma was so shameful that they fear exposing it would make them undesirable, particularly in the case of

s e x u a l abuse-(either person).

2) Talking about it would mean reliving the horrible pain that they swore they would never relive again.

Imagine back in the old cowboy days, riding through the desert and you fall of your horse and break your leg. By the time you get to a doctor, weeks later, your leg has healed. Since it wasn't set properly, the leg is deformed, causing you to walk with a limp-one that by now you have become "comfortable" with.

Sometime later you are made aware of your limp. You go to the doctor and he says that in order to "make you walk properly", he'll have to "re-break" your leg. When you remember the pain of breaking your leg you cry, "No way, I'll never relive that pain again!" I'll just make it as I am. That is often how many handle major traumatic experiences. Your limp is now your new norm, you've adjusted to it.

3) It was so terrible that blocking it from their mind made them actually forget about it altogether, or...

4) They were so young when it happened that their conscience mind actually does not remember it!

That brings me to a horrific, heart-wrenching story an evangelist told about sexual abuse. In a country over-seas, there was a "brothel" that offered children for sex. The story was one where a grown man came into the brothel, consumed some form of demonic alcohol, and proceeded to have sex with an 18-month old baby. Eventually the baby was rescued. Here is the question. Is the child likely to remember it-not likely? Is it going to have an emotional effect on the child as she grows up-most assuredly? But how can it be diagnosed if she doesn't remember it, and no one else knows about it?

As the cycle turns over, we have young people finding themselves in parental roles who were "deprived" of their own childhood. Many times these couples get romantically involved, move in together, have children, but avoid the dreaded "curse" of marriage. In essence, the relationship is not built on a solid foundation, but on one waiting to crumble at life's next thunderstorm.

A former pastor of mine related something he often heard while counseling married couples. One spouse would say, "I'm sorry, that's not the person I married-they have changed.'" His response would usually be, "Oh, that's the person you married alright- it's just not the person you dated."

Some years ago, I saw a documentary on marriage and divorce. One story that stuck with me was related to a short-lived, 6 month marriage. The woman told the story of how she met her husband, fell in love, and they were married six months later. Just after they were married, football season started. He was so totally consumed in football that the wife was almost completely ignored as he went from game to game to game on TV. By the time football season was over, she had had enough and divorced him.

When asked, "Why did you marry a man like that?" Her response was. "It wasn't football season when I was getting to know him-I did not know he was like that."

Obviously, no one is ever going to know absolutely everything about anybody. Nevertheless, there are some basic, essential things that must be laid on the table in order for relationships to be built on solid ground. In no way do I claim to have all of the answers. Hopefully, the few things I have mentioned and the few that follow, will help you cultivate a mindset of the type of things to look for and address.

-When a spot of bitterness or unforgiveness is spotted. People try to hide or lock up that spirit, but in almost every case it can't stand the spotlight of close relationships.

-Acknowledging past trauma but refusing to talk about it. (Usually if a person can't talk about it, they haven't healed sufficiently.)

-Understanding future goals as well as past experiences. For instance, there are certain professions or careers that can make marriage very difficult, and even more so with children. In some cases, people commit "emotional infidelity" by putting their careers ahead of their actual spouse and/or the children. That is very common is professions like sports coaching, "full-time" preaching, musicians, military persons, and law enforcers, just to name a few.

-Parent /child relationships: To the women: In most cases, how a man treats his mother, that's how he will likely treat you."

And last but not least,-time. So often, the real important issues that people have will only be exposed by time.

And by the way, even if marriage is not being considered yet, get the help you need anyway. That emotional healing could go a long way toward enhancing all of the other important relationships in your life.

Obviously, there are many more emotional and trauma related experiences that affect relationships. Some are more obvious and easier to manage or eliminate than others. I am not saying that each person must be at a state of emotional perfection before they get married. What I am saying is this: expose and talk about each one's pathology, get the necessary help in resolving what you know to be "dark spots", and keep working on it until the necessary healing takes place. **Identify, acknowledge, and, take action!**

In the end, this life offers few guarantees, no matter what you do. I believe that we must, as a society, realize that finding true and meaningful relationships are worth the research, risk, time, and the effort. If we can mend the past hurts and become stable within ourselves, we can withstand the disappointments and failures that life can, and almost certainly will, bring.

For so many and for so long, life's tragedies and disappointments has brought so much pain. It has caused people to miss out on the most necessary and fundamental elements that will give us life-faith, hope, and love. For when faith and hope are lost, love has no foundation to build upon. And without love, life is but a sounding brass, and a clanging cymbal. That is why it is so important to find that someone to h e l p lift you out of the muck and mire that life can bring, and keep you going until you reach that ultimate goal.

Love suffers long, and is kind; love doesn't envy; love does not parade itself, and is not puffed up. Love bears all things, hopes all things, and endures all things. And now abide faith, hope and love, these three; but the greatest of these is love. **Love never fails**.

Shhh…Listen

It is my hope that since you have gotten this far in the book, something that has been said has struck a chord with you, or in some way opened your eyes or made sense to you. My quest from this point on is to convince you that I have saved the best, or shall I say perhaps, most important thought, for last.

In all of my writings I make a supreme effort to stress the importance of listening. Hopefully this will fill in any gaps I may have left open. To help you understand how powerful I think it is, I can best do that by explaining its association with what I believe is the most important, powerful, and misunderstood element of our humanity, and that element is called, Love.

It is my belief that we are born with what I might term the "firewood of success", resting deep in our soul. In order for that firewood to ignite and guide us into our destiny, it must be ignited. It is my contention that the element needed to ignite that fire, is love, but the oxygen that makes it burn, is called listening.

When raising a baby who is not able to speak, we listen to its cries, smiles, and other gestures to determine what the child needs at that time. That is the only way a baby can communicate.

As the years roll on and the child is able to speak, we need to "listen more to their actions and reactions to help determine the child's personality, gifting, and to a small degree perhaps, their designed life's destiny. By the beginning of the teen years, this element of listening most likely will become the "elephant in the living room." If that "elephant" is not present at the necessary time, the resulting emotional rampage has the potential to destroy not only the child, but his household, community, and future generations.

A different kind of child abuse?

We all know that child abuse comes in many forms and has many faces. Unfortunately, my experience has led me to believe that the emotional fallout that comes simply from not listening appropriately to the child at the right time and in the right way, often results in emotional abuse that can produce greater damage than some physical abuses.

Now, let me be clear. Listening to your child and sympathizing with his desires does not mean allowing him to have his way in everything. It simply means allowing him to honestly, openly, and properly express himself, and acknowledging that you feel, hear, and understand his concerns. As a parent who cares, you obviously are the one who decides what actions can be accepted and tolerated and what cannot. Give him as much leeway as you know is good and healthy. But the simple fact that he knows that you HEARD him and cared about what he cared about, will give him the sense of acceptance he needs-simply because he knows that you REALLY **listened** to him, and saw his life from "his" perspective. The love and acceptance he now feels will guide him past many of life's emotional pitfalls as he moves on.

When that happens, here's what happens to him. Even though he may not like your answers or decisions, the simple fact that he got to "speak his mind and was heard," makes him feel that he really is loved, and brings a sense of worth because he is being "considered." That is that "cornerstone" block he needs in order to stay on track.

I heard a sermon once entitled, "Are you being considered?" It was centered on the character 'Job' in the Bible. One day when God said to Satan, "Have you considered Job, my faithful servant?" It went on the talk about how God had so much faith in Job that was not afraid to allow Satan to tempt him.

The preacher then compared it to how good it feels to be considered for a promotion at work-even if you weren't the final choice. The fact that you were even considered was enough motivation to move forward whether you got the position or not.

A similar thing happens to your child when at least they know they've been listened to. When your child can talk to you openly, about anything he feels he needs to talk about, it opens the door for honest dialogue. It makes him confident that you see life not only from your perspective, but also from his. (Remember how you were at that age?) He now knows that you understand his feelings, whether you like those feelings or not. To know that someone understands and is sympathetic, (regardless of the subject matter, and regardless if the answer is yes or no), is the main element that fuses the relationship.

That important element will serve as a good foundation for all future conversations. It is likely to be a major factor that allows him to come to you and admit he did something that he knows you are totally against. Even though he knows how much you may abhor his actions, he is confident, whether he's punished or not, that he will be listened to, forgiven, (with or without consequences), and loved. That's the kind of relationship that both parties can flourish in, and what the child desperately needs.

Now, despite the circumstances, and whatever consequences that follows what has happened, there is now a new "elephant", (I mean "spirit)," in the living room…and his name is Love. Love is perhaps the most important flower that blooms from the seed of listening. And I can almost assure you-the next time that son thinks about making a bad choice, he'll will be reminded of the solid love relationship that exists, which is likely to bring about sufficient strength to make the right choices-at least most of the time.

Understand, once they reach those early teen years that is usually the point at which bad decisions, fueled by bad relationships, can open the doors for trouble. This is often the most critical time that those decisions could affect the entire family for years, or even generations to come.

Oh, and one more thing. If for some reason there is difficulty in forging that necessary relationship, seek help by counseling or, dare I say it, find a mentor for your child, or anyone that can become a "parent-child" diplomat. Get it done.

Up to this point, meaning the pre-teen years, the path-of-logic they have traveled has been primarily one that the parents have forged. From this point on, each child has the ability to forge, or re-direst their own path. They will use those past experiences and relationships as their roadmap.

** I might as well take this space to share my own experience, one of not feeling loved. I grew up in a large family, and I was the last child of eleven children. All in all I had a wonderful childhood and grew up in a good neighborhood and environment. Outside of the normal, occasional teasing by my siblings, there were mostly good relationships among us. I can honestly say that I never felt abused or treated unfairly. I harbored no dislike or hatred for anyone in my family.*

For no reason I could think of, around the age of 5 I began to feel as though no one loved me. Well, this puzzled me greatly because I could not understand to source of that ill feeling. So, from early on in grade school, my daily mission was to find a girlfriend, someone to love me. (Yes, even at five years old)!

That continued on throughout High School and college. I spent many agonizing nights trying to figure out why I felt that way. There was no tangible memory or experience I could pin it on. It was a secret agony that tormented me daily, but who could I tell, what would I say? I literally had no explanation for the emptiness I felt, but rest assured it was an agonizing, relentless emptiness.

Here is the real irony! I eventually did get married, and it was nearly two years after marriage and becoming a Christian, that the mystery was solved!

While walking to catch the bus to work, early one dark

morning, I experienced a conversation with God that blew my mind to the point that I almost started cursing in response! As plain as the pavement I was walking on, I believe God said to me, "the reason you never have felt loved growing up is that no one really KNOWS YOU! He said, no one has put in the time and effort to really, really listen to you, your heart, and what is important to you. Thus no one truly understands you and the treasures I put in your heart.

-If I may interrupt this message for an important announcement-

Enter the Mentor

As a child approaches those teenage years, it is most likely the time to consider introducing a mentor into their life, if not before. That mentor, largely because of the stage of life they are in, can help close the gap between the mindsets of the two "warring parties." On one hand he is young enough to relate to and support the teenager, yet mature enough to see the parental position.

In my experience, I have had to be that mediator and peacemaker between two warring parties and here is the tricky part: YOU CAN'T TAKE SIDES! The parent must have the confidence in the mindset and integrity of the mentor, and the child must believe that the mentor will go to bat for him, in the appropriate way. Many times, the mentee will accept the direction and advice from the mentor, which ultimately was the same mindset of the parent! Sometimes, though the message is the same, the source makes the difference!

-Commercial over, proceed-

<u>No one can love you intimately if they don't really know you, and cherish your thoughts, dreams, and aspirations-regardless of what they are.</u> He went on to say, that's how I know you love Me, because by studying my word I know that you cherish what is important to me, which affects how you relate to me, and that equates to you really "knowing" me. Though you can have a general and true love for people in general, the personal, close, relationships will be bonded by another level of intimacy. You can really like a person whole lot, but crossing that threshold to love means that you value that person's thoughts and everything about them as much or more than your own.

*In a sense, in a true marriage, each party "surrenders" themselves to the other one, putting their well-being and fulfillment ahead of their own. If you believe the story of the gospel, that's how you know that God, in Jesus, loves you.**

Needless to say, I was blown away. But I was blown to the place I needed to be, a place where the relationship with my Heavenly Father and I could begin to be solidified.

Okay, where was I. Oh yeah, the culminating of relationships lies in really, truly, knowing one another, brought about by truly **listening to one another, and respecting and accepting how the other person feels**.

As a parent, this in no way relinquishes your status as head of the household and maker of the rules, (and enforcing them). However, I believe that if you can manage to build a good habit of "listening relationships" with your children, I can almost assure you that you will have less trouble, more comradery, better relationships, and most of all, more peace in your home.

When I begin a mentoring relationship with a young man, my first goal is establishing a trust upon which a solid relationship can be built. That means getting to truly know one another. That takes sufficient time, and truly being honest and LISTENING to one another.

Then I can move to the next phase of getting him to tell me everything he NEEDS to tell me, in order for me to help him sort out where he is in life, and become the man he was destined to be. There are three avenues that I must travel as I go down his life's past: 1)watching his actions, 2) truly listening to the things he says, and sometimes more importantly, 3) listening to his heart to capture the things I need to hear that he "can't", is ashamed of, or doesn't know how to say. (That is obviously a challenge).

As a parent, mentor, or any kind of therapist, I believe that mastering the art of listening is the most important skill of all. No matter what "cures" one may have, unless there is the sufficient skill of listening in place, it is likely not going to produce the understanding and proper treatment (response) that is needed.

I have had experiences with mentees that when that moment comes and they feel assured that I have listened, understood, and accepted them as they are, and where they are, our relationship shifts into another gear. Typically, that's when they begin to feel loved and cared for, and their outlook on life usually begins to change.

At this point, have I solved all of their problems?-Of course not. But what has happened is that now they are emotionally strengthened, better equipped to manage the heavy emotional baggage that is dragging them down, and most importantly, ready to reveal the haunting secrets that need sharing. They also know that there is a place, a person they can come to when that next obstacle is in the way. Knowing that someone cares and understands leads to what most traumatized people are missing: a strong, committed relationship of hope, strength, and love. It is a fundamental part of the foundation on which successful and meaningful lives and relationships are built-and restored.

Now, for you adults who have been living with bottled-up, hidden, painful secrets, it's your turn. Once you come to the realization and understanding that you are ready for your inner healing, here is perhaps your biggest problem-deciding to talk about your trauma.

Remember, talking means exposing the hidden areas of pain that makes you uncomfortable and vulnerable, often exposing something embarrassing and or shameful. You realize that you must get "emotionally naked", ready to accept the humility that may result from the honesty that you dread to face, but knowing that it is a necessary part of the healing process.

You basically have two options- a close, trusted and knowledgeable friend, or a professional therapist. Many who can afford and have access to a therapist choose that because it feels "safer." Either way, the only way to "save your soul", as it were, is to become completely transparent and honest about your trauma. For most, that is the most difficult step- but of course, it is the most important.

Either way, the platform is now laid for the emotional surgery that must take place.

Listening is the doorway to Love.

A New Program

As we are now in the "computer age", everything done on a computer is based on the way it is programmed. I'm sure we've all heard the comparison that our brains are "computers" of a sort. Well guess what, that means that they get programmed, too. The program starts the day we are born (actually it can happen in the womb), and, it never really stops.

Well, just like a computer, what goes in our programmed brains will largely determine what comes out, directly affecting the area of emotions. When it comes to discussing why some people consistently repeat bad, destructive, and criminal behavior, that programming is usually front and center. Although there is no one reason that applies to all situations, usually the decisions they make can be traced back to that "programming" history.

I believe the saying is, "garbage in-garbage out." (Or, something like that). From early childhood, emotional ups and downs are being slotted in the human psyche. Depending what slots are filled with normal, healthy experiences, or unhealthy experiences, so goes the brain, as it begins processing that information and placing it in its appropriate slot.

Much emotional damage in the formative years can begin with something as simple as not being held and touched as a baby, all the way to physical instability, abuse, and unhealthy environments.

Since the brain is such a protective force, it taps into each person's network of defenses to compensate for the unpleasant, unnatural, or harmful experiences. The end result is often negative or anti-social behavior. If the situation and the emotional responses continue, a pattern of behavior is established, creating a "program" of behavior that it deems is necessary for feeling better or safer, or simply for survival. At some point, the behavior eventually deems itself not only appropriate and "comfortable", but normal.

Now your inborn computer has created a new, "acceptable" form of behavior-a new program. Seldom, if ever, does that old program "correct itself. It usually doesn't "correct itself" just because a person gets older.

In computers, often a new hard drive must be inserted in order to get different results. In a sense, the (brain) computer must be re-programmed.

Just as the computer must be receptive to read the new program from the new disk, so too, must the individual be receptive to its new programming. This reprogramming usually begins with dialogue between the counselor/mentor/therapist. In most cases, the person being re-programmed needs to have a comfortable relationship with the person doing the reprogramming; otherwise they may not be receptive at all. That is simply human nature.

When its' all said and done, I believe that one of, if not the most important element, in redirecting one's pathology and healing of the resulting emotional wounds is uncovering the past, no matter how painful, horrific, or depressing it might be. It is likely the only way you will understand why you are the way you are. Your life has left a trail of emotional road(s) that got you where you are today. The amount of success you will have in getting your mind, emotions, and life on the right path is directly related to how well you identify, re-pave, redirect, or simply shut down the roads that led you to where you are. Unfortunately for many, simply identifying and retracing those roads will not be enough. Those are likely to be the most painful and the biggest challenges. Somewhere, somehow, you must convince yourself that the end result will be worth the pain and effort to do so. In most cases, you need someone you really trust to take that journey with you, to hold your hand, steady your stride, and to help you take the next step when the fear or pain begins to overwhelm you.

If you begin to doubt that the pain and effort is worth it, remember, this work is not just for you, but also for those who you love, the ones that love you, as well as the ones who may need your help to redirect their paths.

Identify your road(s), or if necessary, add yours:
Abandonment
Abuse (sexual, physical, psychological…)
Degradation
Bullying
A destroyed self-esteem
Feeling Unloved or unwanted

And, you fill in "your" blank:

____

____

____

____

____

Now, the next step is up to you. Will you take it or stay put?

The Monster(s) Within

I recently saw an episode of Criminal Minds, and as is typical, each episode ends with a "life quote." This one struck a chord with me, and unfortunately it is much too close to reality. It speaks directly to the pathology in each and every one of us. It goes like this:

"I believe in monsters, and I believe in ghosts. We all have them lurking inside of us...and sometimes they win."

The emotional and psychological monsters that torment us are deceptive, strong, and powerful. The pains, frustrations, abuses, disappointments, and the rest of the evil, deadly emotions that sometimes are seemingly endless, are constantly at our doorstep. They are relentless, and seek to completely consume us.

These monsters are the pains from the trauma, disappointments, and abuses that reside deep in our souls that haunt us, seeking to destroy the foundations we need in order to build strong, meaningful, and successful relationships-which are the foundations of a healthy, fulfilled life. At the end of the day, the biggest elephant, or maybe I should say, "Goliath", in the living room, is the missing love, resulting from damaged or missing relationships.

All of the other traumas, as painful as they may be, are just "tag-alongs". Nevertheless, there is a formula to defeat Goliath, as well as his four other friends. Just as victory resided in the five stones in David's slingshot pouch, so to do we have "five smooth stones," stones that we can use to take down our emotional monsters. It is life's monsters that surround us by destroying or damaging the necessary pillars of strength you needed to have. The five smooth stones for your healing are listening, understanding, acceptance, forgiveness, and love, and may be described this way:

Listening-now I know that you understand how I really feel.

Understanding-Now you really **know** why I am the way I am.

Acceptance-Regardless of my past, you still believe that I have value, and am worth loving.

Forgiveness-Accepting my frailties and youthfulness, and giving me another chance.

Love -And at the end of the day,
I will know that I am loved. **That is the stone that landed dead center in Goliath's forehead. For when your Goliath falls and love makes its home in your heart, nothing or no one can stand against you.**

Now I have the healthy, emotional relationship(s) I need in order to not only to survive, but to thrive. It is my new path…oh come on, let me say it, my new "pathology" that is going to bring wholeness and healing to myself, and those I touch.

Unfortunately, there will be some who read this, understand it, and even believe healing can be attained. They believe that what has been presented is not only doable, but have a strong assurance that it will work, but they won't do it. Why? because most will not be able to gather the strength to relive the pain and trauma. Some don't believe they have the support system (or the "right" friend to lean on). Some have lived with it so long that they have decided that the "possible" healing is simply no longer worth the painful journey that they foresee. For a few, they have adjusted to their trauma, and no longer see it as something to be changed, and just decide to live with it.

Perhaps the most unfortunate consequence of those decisions will result in them transferring their pain and trauma on to the next generation-not even realizing they are doing it.

-I pray that you don't let your monsters win.-

Mentoring Dynamics

Mentoring: The dynamics involved when an adult male comes alongside a young man to provide a powerful and important role model. As humans, particularly young ones, the core values we learn are more modeled than spoken. I believe the saying is, "More is *caught* than *taught*." These role models' primary goals are to be that all-important listening ear, and that caring and needed companion who imparts valuable life lessons and relationship skills. It is upon these elements that a relationship of trust and commitment is formed. The personal healing that is experienced by having someone truly listen to and empathize with you is without equal. That, along with a feeling of acceptance without judgment is at the heart of helping a hurting and traumatized person to a place of emotional well-being.

At the end of the day that relationship serves to bridge the gap created by the "missing" parent or caregiver. It begins to restore the emotional/psychological void that has a profound effect on the young man's self-esteem, decision-making process, and thus, his future. That self-esteem will help to be a springboard for everything that young person seeks to achieve in life. Mentoring relationships can last several months, years, or decades- and the outcome, a lifetime.

Interaction between mentor and mentee may include many forms of communication and activities. Those activities can range from board games, to videos/movies, or to religious discussions. When it is all said and done, the trust, faith, and camaraderie that results is the heart and soul of what a youth needs in order to restore the faith that is the foundation of his existence and purpose.

As touched on earlier, I suspect we all know by now that the genesis of most of the destructive pathology in our communities is the single-parent home, followed closely by the two-parent dysfunctional home, topped off with a dysfunctional environment (neighborhood). I believe this is primarily a relationship problem that is fed by several entities, primarily our failing to recognize the importance of family structure, the pathology of our communities, the media, etc. Consequently, I believe that this type of intervention is the first and most important step in stemming that tide. The totality of these mentoring elements will inevitably assist the mentee in being a better person, and likely a better father himself, leading to breaking that chain of family dysfunction.

To my knowledge, the standing protocol for most organizations is to match one mentor to one mentee. Unfortunately, there aren't, and likely never will be, enough mentors to meet the one-on-one relationship that I believe is optimal. What we are left with is the dynamics of "group mentoring". This can be facilitated by movies/videos, or book materials. It would basically be an open forum discussion guided by the needs expressed by the group (as appropriate). That type of forum will pave the way to opportunities for one-on-one, "heart-to heart" sessions.

That is the foundation I believe we need to start from in order to turn the tide in our sons, our families, our communities, and our society.

May God bless you, all.

No words necessary.

The Pathology of Emotions